ROAD TRANSPORT
WALES & BORDER

by
Paul Heaton

P.M. Heaton Publishing
Abergavenny Monmouthshire
Great Britain
2005

Front Cover: A Scania tractor unit and curtainsider semi-trailer owned by Lloyds of Ludlow shown negotiating Ludlow's ancient River Bridge.

Frontispiece: Three units of the B.W. Rees & Son fleet fitted for milk churn collection, two Bedford 'O' type vehicles EBO994 and FTX865 with a Bedford OWLD, HTG983.

Pages 4 & 5: The fleet of H.S. Williams, Whitchurch, Ross-on-Wye is shown outside the Crown Hotel and Tower Stores, Whitchurch, just prior to nationalisation. Pictured with the vehicles are (from the left) George Thomas, Bernard Phillips, Charlie Morris, Neville Williams (son of owner), Horace Williams (owner), Fred Morgan, Don Winters and Ken Edmonds.

Back Cover: Foden 6x2 tractor unit W159UCJ and bulk tipper semi-trailer owned by Roberts Transport (Ross Roadways), of Whitchurch, Ross-on-Wye.

ISBN 1 872006 20 5
© First Edition October, 2005

Published by P.M. Heaton Publishing
Abergavenny, Monmouthshire, NP7 8NG

Printed in Great Britain by
The Amadeus Press Ltd.,
Cleckheaton, West Yorkshire, BD19 4TQ

Typesetting and page layout by
Highlight Type Bureau Ltd., Bradford BD8 7BY

CONTENTS

Roy Smith who served with Lloyds of Ludlow for 44 years is seen with a Scania 113M, index number F688BNY.

PREFACE

In this further volume in my 'Road Transport' series I have featured businesses based in Shropshire, Herefordshire, Gloucestershire and Cardiff. Whilst involved in a wide variety of traffic, including general haulage, steel traffic, bulk tippers, animal feedstuffs and livestock transport, much space is devoted to milk collections both in churn and bulk. All these firms hauled into and out of South Wales, whilst B.W. Rees & Son, were to be found operating over a much wider area than their Welsh base would suggest. An international dimension is introduced with Lloyds of Ludlow's participation in transport throughout the Continent and North Africa.

I am grateful to all those who have helped in the compilation of this book, including Nick Cole, Robin Harris, Norman Lloyd, Tony Lloyd, Michael Parry, Graham Rees, Anthony Roberts, Graham Roberts, Haydn Roberts and Terry Roberts. To anyone else who has helped – thank you.

To the reader, I hope you enjoy this further look back in time.

Paul Heaton
Abergavenny
October, 2005

This ERF 'E' Series tractor unit L510JBE was operated by B. M. Cole & Sons.

B.M. COLE & SONS, WELSH NEWTON

Brothers Bert Matthew and Frank Cole were in business as haulage contractors from the late 1940s and were mainly involved in livestock transport. I remember in the 1960s Frank operating from Monmouth, whilst Bert was based at The Garage, Welsh Newton. Bert had three sons, Matthew, Nick and Simon, and eventually the business was involved in general haulage trading as B.M. Cole & Sons. Sadly in 1976 Bert died at the early age of 57. The firm was carried on, and the three brothers each drove a vehicle. Tragically Nick was injured, not whilst driving, and had to give up HGV driving. Today, Matthew and Simon each drive an ERF 'E' series 6x2 tractor unit, and are involved in steel transport out of South Wales, and bulk tipper work usually on scrap.

Their base at Welsh Newton is situated on the road from Monmouth to Hereford, just a few hundred yards inside Herefordshire.

This 6x2 ERF EC11 tractor unit R849RDM is parked at the Welsh Newton premises of B. M. Cole & Sons.

In the upper picture it is shown laden with steel coils.

This ERF articulated tractor unit and bulk tipping trailer R549DNE, is operating on hauling scrap.

LLOYDS OF LUDLOW

Norman Thomas Lloyd was born on August 12, 1908. His father was a clerk with the Clee Hill Quarry out side Ludlow, and was eventually manager of their Titterston Quarry. When Norman left school he went to work in the quarry but by the late 1920s he was in partnership, operating two Chevrolet dropside lorries, one four wheeler and a six wheeler. Based in Birmingham they used these vehicles in delivering Hercules pedal cycles, from the manufacturer to bicycle dealers and other outlets. This venture was not successful, they dissolved it, and thereafter he returned to Ludlow, where he vowed never to go into partnership ever again.

In 1931 Oxford Bye-pass was being constructed and Clee Hill Quarry provided much of the stone needed. As a result Clee Hill bought four six wheelers for the job, all tippers. Two Leyland Hippo's both petrol-engined, and two AEC one petrol-engined, and the other diesel-powered. Norman drove one of the Leylands'. Like a number of the drivers, he was booked for speeding through Tleobury Mortimer, and he was a bit put out when he lost a half-days pay, to appear before a Special Court at Bewdley.

Dick Davies of Ludlow had two stock lorries, both with carrier's licenses which he parked at the Queen's Head public house in Ludlow. He wanted to dispose of them, and although only one was in sufficiently good condition to use Norman paid his deposit. Thereafter he went home and persuaded his parents to lend him the balance. Thus on May 12, 1937 he started up in business with a Commer 4-wheeler, and a Dodge 4-wheeler, on livestock transport, and regularly attended markets at Hereford, Ludlow, Craven Arms, Bishops Castle, Leominster, Bidgnorth, Tenbury Wells, Kidderminster, Kington, Knighton, and horse sales at Cheltenham. As he expanded he became involved on milk churn collections from local farms.

During the Second World War he was appointed Centre Foreman at Ludlow and Craven Arms cattle markets, and organised the haulage and allocation of work at these two locations.

The nature of his work meant that he avoided nationalisation in 1949, particularly as the Road Haulage Executive had counted the single lorry he had working for the NAAFI as employed on furniture transport.

Originally operating out of a yard at Sandpits Road, Ludlow, in 1949 he obtained additional premises when he bought the Temeside Garage, Temeside, Ludlow, which had a Standard-Triumph dealership, which he quickly changed to a Vauxhall-Bedford agency. This business was kept until sold in 1964.

Around 1954 he started carrying cattle feeds from Liverpool on behalf of a local corn merchant back to Ludlow. This was an important source of employment, and he soon secured outward work. There were three sawmills in Ludlow and he obtained loads of timber, but more regularly barrel-staves, for delivery to the brewing industry, at Burton-on-Trent, Liverpool and Glasgow. If the vehicle was in position to load cattle feeds at Liverpool back to Ludlow, all well and good. If however there was nothing on offer, he tried to get a load into South Wales if possible, and thereafter started loading out of South Wales for the Midlands and North from Ebbw Vale, Port Talbot, the Orb at Newport, Whitehead Iron & Steel at Newport, and subsequently Llanwern. This involved considerable expansion and the increase in size of particular vehicles. Livestock haulage was maintained, grain, sugar beat and fertilizer continued to be carried.

Norman's son Tony joined the business from school in 1955, and his sisters Christine and Pamela worked in the office until they married.

His first articulated outfit arrived in 1954, this was an ex-British Road Services ERF with a single axle Dyson trailer, ETX930, which was permanently coupled. This was soon replaced with a Maudslay with a tandem axle trailer. However during the Suez crisis, with the reduction of available fuel and rationing, he took it off the road, using its fuel to keep other units of the fleet going. In October, 1959 the first new articulated tractor unit arrived, an AEC Mandator TUX271 which operated at 24 tons GVW.

In 1964 an AEC Mandator Mk.5 AUX192V arrived together with an AEC Mercury AUX193V, and thereafter two AEC tilt-cabbed tractor units – HAW100D and GUX718D, both of which eventually went to Spiers of Melksham. Thereafter a series of Gardner-engined tractor units arrived – Guy, Foden, ERF and Atkinson.

In 1971 he was asked to deliver a load of agricultural machinery to a Paris Show for a regular local customer. This did not require a permit. However they soon needed some, as they expanded into Europe, at first hauling tyres to Zurich, and lard back to the United Kingdom for the baking industry. This had been the first real job on the continent, but from the mid-1970s they were hauling to and from Italy, Germany, France and North Africa, and eventually were carrying out more work overseas than in the United Kingdom.

In 1979 they acquired a Daf agency with a business at Coleshill, Birmingham, but by 1988 had sold it when the merger took place between Leyland and Daf.

By the late 1980s they could no longer compete with continental hauliers and eventually ran this part of the business down to concentrate on UK traffic. This meant a cut in vehicles from their all-time high of 58 tractor units with substantially more semi-trailers.

Whilst operating a number of continental makes – Volvo and Daf, they have standardised now on Scania, and operate a substantial fleet. Whilst Norman could be said to have retired he still takes an interest in the business, having reached 97 years. Son Tony has four daughters – Alison, Susan, Joanne and Elizabeth. Of which Alison and Joanne work part time in the business and Elizabeth the youngest is full time. They operate out of Corve Street, Ludlow, and have appointed a transport manager, Colin Vickress, whose grandfather drove for Lloyds.

Long-serving drivers are Roy Smith (1958-2002), Geoffrey Richards, Tony Ashbridge, Brian Mulliner, Emlyn Evans, Tim Beazley, Doug Turner, Russell Francis and Dave (Oxo) Lewis and Norman Taylor.

Tony Lloyd is an enthusiastic preservationist of commercial vehicles and has an important fleet of restored AEC and Maudslay vehicles.

Above: Shown around 1946 from the left – Leyland Cub, EVT206, Dodge and Austin with stock boxes and Maudslay Mogul 2 DVJ65.

Left: Maudslay Mogul 2, DVJ65 fitted for milk churn collection.

Right: Bought new in 1948 this Maudslay Mogul 3 EAW102 with bodywork by J. H. Thorne & Son was equipped to operate as a dropside or for livestock. The vehicle had the chassis number: 40047.

Seen loading agricultural machinery at McConnell's Factory at Ludlow is this Maudslay 6wl (twin steer) dropside EVJ67? time she was fitted with a new Homalloy cab. With the chassis nu

...ost new from other owners the vehicle was originally a Mogul 3 four-wheeler, and was converted by Lloyds. At the same ...nly one higher than EAW103, they must have been built together.

Opposite: This Maudslay Maharanee articulated outfit JAL604 was loading grain at Marston Bros. Mill at Ludlow en-route to Southampton for shipment to France due to a crop failure.

Overleaf: This Bedford 'S' type HUX878 is fitted with a detachable stockbox built by Vincent Greenhous.

Above: The Maudslay Mogul 3, EAW102, now shown after being fitted with a new cab by Homalloy.

Pages 18/19: This four-wheeler OUX57 is badged as a Maudslay Mercury, as apposed to an AEC, which it clearly is. Norman Lloyd had always been a fan of the Maudslay, obviously ordering the vehicle as such.

Above: This AEC Majestic (twin-steer) 6wl flat TWU789 is fitted with a removable bulk grain carrier.

Below: The same vehicle operating as a drawbar outfit.

Top: Bedford 'S' and 'J' type dropside lorries in the Lloyd's yard.

Centre: Bedford TK surrounded by livestock vehicles.

Bottom: AEC Marshall 6wl tipper fitted with fold-down body.

Above: Lloyds of Ludlow AEC Matador recovery vehicle.

Below: The same vehicle having recovered a Mk3 AEC Mammoth Major to the Temeside Garage at Ludlow.

Above: AEC 6WL recovery vehicle.

Below: The AEC having recovered a Pickfords AEC Mammoth Major Mk.5 and brought it back to the Temeside Garage.

In October, 1958, Lloyds of Ludlow acquired their first new articulated tractor unit. This was an AEC Mandator TUX271. The vehicle operated at 24 tons GVW., and was normally coupled to a 4-in-line semi trailer, as seen below. Roy Smith and Tony Lloyd are seen standing by the vehicle.

Above: TUX271 is seen outside the Temeside Garage loaded with charcoal destined for Heysham.
Below: TUX271 loaded with barrel staves for the brewing industry.

In 1964 Norman Lloyd bought this AEC Mandator tractor unit AUX192B which is shown loaded with soft drinks.

This AEC Mercury tractor unit AUX193B seen operating with a stock box was bought at the same time as the Mandator.

This 1966 Commer two-stroke tractor unit FNT637D is loaded with fire bricks from Scotland.

Shown new this Seddon 4wl dropside was often used with a livestock box, serving local cattle markets.

A 1965 Commer two-st

transporter CUX145C.

Four articulated outfits, Guy, two AEC Egromatic-cabbed Mandators' GUX718D and HUX100D and a
Mk.5Mandator AUX192B.

Driver Harry Grant is seen with the 1966 AEC Mandator GUX718D.

Around a dozen Guy Big 'J' tractor units were operated. They were fitted with Gardner 6LXB (180) engine.

This 1967 Foden KAW400E is shown loaded for Scotland.

Lloyds of Ludlow had always favoured the Maudslay and later AEC model. From the mid-1960s they had based their heavier vehicles on the Gardner 180 (6LXB) engine, in a Guy Invincible, Guy Big 'J', and Foden chassis. Later they operated two Atkinson Borderer tractor units fitted with the Gardner 240 (8LXB) engine. Thereafter they bought Continental tractor units – Scania, Volvo F86, F88 and F12 and Daf. The first foreign vehicle acquired was a Scania 110 in 1969. An Atkinson, Volvo F86, Volvo F88 and Scania 110 are shown together (above).
Below: a line of Volvo F86 and F88 tractor units are shown.

In 1971 they started operating to the Continent and for two decades were carrying out more work abroad than in the United Kingdom.

Above: Three Volvo F88 outfits are shown at the Muttenz Custom Terminal at Basle, Switzerland in 1972.

Below: Volvo F88 BAW308L is stopped at the Muttenz Terminal.

Opposite top: Seven Daf tractor units operated by Lloyds of Ludlow. The first Daf arrived in the fleet in 1976. In 1979 they obtained a Daf agency with a business in Coleshill, Birmingham.

Opposite centre: Daf tractor units RNT316R, RUJ426R and RUJ427R.

Opposite bottom: A Scania 111 and six Volvo F12 tractor units undercover.

Above: Two Dafs and a Scania parked up in snow on the Italian side of Mont Blanc Tunnel in 1980. (Restaurant "Des Amis" Lilla-Quart).

Overleaf: A Scania 111 – YUX556T carrying steelwork on an extendable trailer.

This Daf HAW840V is shown operating as a low-loa

new Hymac machine from Rhymney in South Wales.

Daf 3300 6x2 tractor unit D88SNT.

Daf 6x4 tractor unit with a semi-trailer finished in a customers livery.

Four Scania 113M 6x2 tractor units with consecutive index number: F53BUJ-F56BUJ.

Three, Scania 113M outfits, F23DUJ, F54BUJ and F24DUJ refuelling at a Service Area at Ghent, Belgium. The vehicles were loaded with heating elements en-route from Kidderminster to Traunreut, Southern Germany.

Scania 113M tractor unit F53 BUJ with a van trailer.

Scania 113M tractor unit F55BUJ with a tandem-axle curtainsider trailer.

Leyland Daf tractor unit G333HNT with the only Mercedes to be owned by Lloyds of Ludlow – G910PVJ.

Two Scania 113M tractor units coupled to trailers in the livery of customer E. Walters (Ludlow) Ltd. These were used for goods conveyed to Tangier in North Africa.

Scania 113M P223ANT with a step-frame tri-axle trailer.

Scania 124L tractor units R271UUJ and R272UUJ.

Long serving drivers Roy Smith and Godfrey Richards with Norman Lloyd infront of Scania T421JAW and the preserved AEC Mandator TUX271.
The new Scania was Roy's latest vehicle. He had driven the AEC from new forty years earlier.

Modern Scania 124L tractor unit DX51JUK.

PRESERVED AND RESTORED VEHICLES

Index No.	Vehicle	History/Notes
EMP164	AEC Mammoth Major Mk. 2 8wl dropside	1936 new to Tile Haulage, Middlesex; thence to Yandle & Bishop, Somerset; and then Perry & Perry, Beaminster, Dorset; Acquired from West of England Transport Collection at Winkleigh, in 1977 and restored. This vehicle was the 150th Mammoth Major built.
HHT184	AEC Mammoth Major Mk. 2 8wl dropside	1941 new to William Butler, Bristol, as a tanker; later turned into a flat as a showman's vehicle; Acquired from Dave Hoare, Chepstow, and restored.
EP9329	Maudslay Mogul 2 4wl dropside	1946 new to H.V. Bowen & Sons, New Mills, Newtown, Powys, from whom acquired in 1981 and restored.
JAC21	Maudslay Mogul 3 4wl flat	1949 new to Flower's Brewery, Stratford-on-Avon; 1981 acquired from an Oxfordshire Showman and restored.
KXU781	Maudslay Meritor 8wl dropside	1949 new to British Road Services, Nottingham; Acquired from a scrap yard near Luton and restored. This vehicle was one of about 250 of this type built.
DYE944C	AEC Mammoth Major Mk.5 8wl flat	1965 new to Watney, Coombe & Reid, Mortlake Brewery, London as a brewery tanker; passed to Danters, Showmen of Gloucester, who extended the wheelbase by 10ft in order to transport dodgems; Acquired in 1990 and restored. Vehicle put back to original wheelbase.
TUX271	AEC Mandator Mk. 3 articulated tractor unit	10.1959 new to Lloyds of Ludlow; restored in 2000. This vehicle fitted with a Homalloy cab, operated at 24 tons GVW.
FAW122C	AEC Mammoth Major Mk. 5 6wl flat	1965 new to Ministry of Supply; 1981 to timber haulier Gartland of Droitwich, who used for ten years, and vehicle then stood for a further ten; 2001 acquired, registered and restored.

Now preserved by Tony Lloyd, AEC Mammoth Major Mk. 2, HHT184 is shown new in 1941 as delivered to William Butler, Bristol as a tanker.

Top left: Shown preserved, this AEC Mandator TUX271 was bought new in 1958, and was their first new articulated vehicle.

Above: Seven of the Lloyds of Ludlow preserved fleet.

Left: Norman Lloyd is shown with the preserved vehicles. AEC Mammoth Major Mk.2, 8wl dropside – EMP164. AEC Mammoth Major Mk. 2, 8wl dropside – HHT184. Maudslay Mogul 2, 4wl dropside – EP9329. Maudslay Mogul 3, 4wl flat – JAC21.

Maudslay Meritor 8wl dropside – KXU781

AEC Mandator tractor unit – TUX271

AEC Mammoth Major Mk.5, 8wl flat, DYE944C.

Overleaf: Pictured infront of the AEC Mammoth Major EMP164 ready to leave Ludlow for London in May 1978 for the London-Brighton H.C.V.S. Run.

From left: Mechanic Charlie Ashbridge, Tony Lloyd, Glyn Swain, Dave Webster and John Boughey.

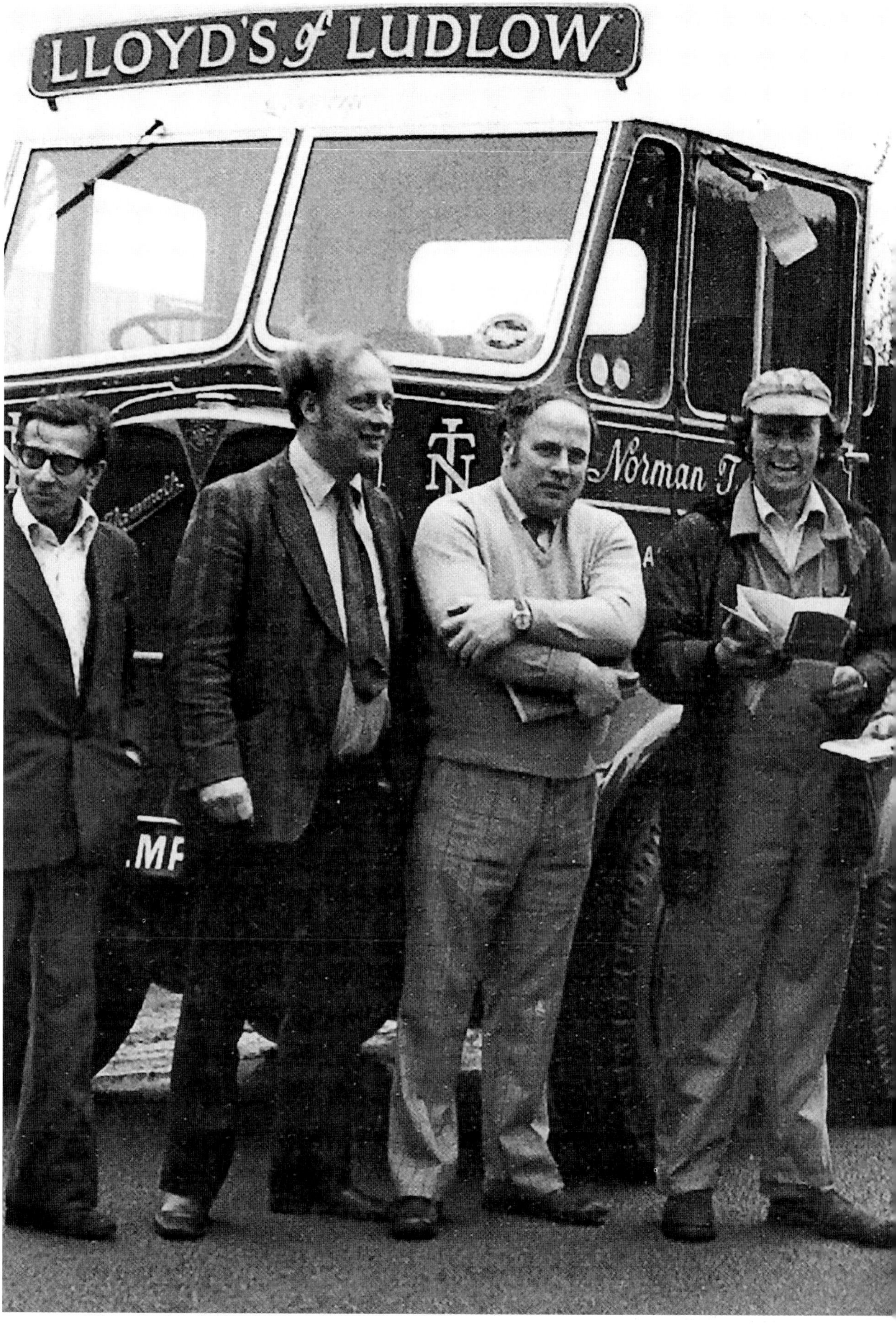
LLOYD'S of LUDLOW
Norman T

WM. PARRY & SONS, ST. BRIAVELS

William Parry, who lived at Little Hoggins, Coleford Road, St. Briavels, started in business on his own account in 1935, as a live stock and general haulage contractor, but also selling and delivering coal and timber. His father Walter had been a timber tusher (pulling timber out of the woods with a horse and chains) and carrying it by horse and cart to sawmills. William had initially helped his father, but set out on his own when he was 26 years of age.

He expanded in November, 1947 when the garage and adjoining house – East Villa in St. Briavels was bought, and thereafter sold petrol and carried out motor repairs. Another incentive to purchasing this business was that it included a four wheeled lorry with an 'A' Carriers License.

Expansion continued and household removals and car hire were added to his range of work. Some of his early lorries included a Bedford VJ9111, a Seddon GDF624 in 1946 and an Albion CTV924 from Watts of Lydney.

Sadly in 1963 he died at the early age of 54, and the running of the business passed to his sons John (26 years old) and 22 year old Michael. Initially times were difficult, but eventually they succeeded in expanding and brought their fleet up to nine vehicles. They were involved in a wide range of activities, including motor repairs, petrol sales, car hire, general haulage, livestock transport, milk churn collections, household removals, timber, animal feedstuffs – bagged and in bulk, and operated two small lorries owned by Daylay Eggs. Daylay had numerous poultry farms in the area and an Egg Packing Station at Monmouth, and Parry's were responsible for providing drivers and for maintenance.

The firm's current business includes the Filling Station, and the transport of livestock, together with the haulage of feedstuffs for BOCM Pauls. Thus 2005 marks the 70th anniversary of the founding of this respected family venture.

SHEEPCOT FARM, TIDENHAM

4 miles from Chepstow, off main Chepstow-Coleford road.

Under instructions from Mr. GEORGE BURFORD, who is relinquishing owing to ill-health,

DAVIS & SONS

Will conduct an unreserved Sale of the whole of the Live and Dead Farming Stock, on the Premises, on

ON THURSDAY, JUNE 29th, 1939

Including :

6 young Deep Milking DAIRY COWS

All lately calved or springing.

SHIRE BRED MARE, 9 years old, good worker in all gears.

PORKER PIG, YOUNG SHEEP DOG.

132 HEAD OF FOWLS (70 Young Laying Hens and Pullets, 62 Black Leghorn, Rhode Island, and Ancona Chicken).

8 Stock Ducks and Drake.

IMPLEMENTS, MACHINES, &c.

2 Ransome Ploughs, 2 Sets Drags, Horse Hoe, Cambridge Roller, Spring Tine and Chain Harrows, Corn Drill, Reaping Machine, Albion Mowing Machine, Mowing Machine (Bamford) Horse Rake, Swath Turner (Bamford), large Galvanised Iron Cattle Crib, Galvanised Sheep Dip in good order, new Sheep Shearing Machine (Wolseley), Grindstone and frame, Clipper Chaff Machine (hand or power), Root Cutter (as new) B.W. Tip Cart, 2 old Wagons, handy Float Cart, Sets of Long, Short, G.O. and Float Harness, 16-rung Ladder, Harvesting and Stable Tools, Bloodless Castrator, Dairy Utensils, Lister Milk Cooler, 40-gallon Lister Separator (as new), End-over-end Churn, Butter Tub, Iron and Stone Pig Troughs, 4 large Portable Fowl Houses, Hebditch Incubator (120 egg), Brooders and Runs, Old Iron, 2 Cider Casks, Gent's Bicycle, Oil Cooking Stove, etc.

SALE AT 2 O'CLOCK.

Auctioneers' Offices : Bank Street, Chepstow.

Davies & Roberts, Ltd., Printers, 26a High Street, Chepstow.

Left: Part of William Parry's business was to attend Farm Dispersal Sales in order to transport livestock, implements and machinery on behalf of buyers. He attended this sale on June 29, 1939, at Sheepcot Farm, Tidenham.

Opposite top: This Austin 4 wheeler was operated on milk churn collection by Wm. Parry & Sons.

Opposite bottom: This Austin dropside DDD210C was normally used delivering animal feedstuffs.

53

Commer articulated outfit KFH333D laden with round timber.

Leyland 4wl flat EDG270L.

This Leyland Badger articulated outfit RUH79H is laden with 'cow kennels' being transported from South Wales to Aberdeen Docks for onward shipping to the Scottish Islands. Jim Harris drove this vehicle. His father served Parry's for 36 years.

These bells were transported from St. Mary's Church, St. Briavels to Uttoxeter for refurbishment. They were conveyed on the Volvo DKR31Y by Parry's as a gesture.

Robin Harris drove the Daf livestock lorry D136SRR for many years. Robin's father and three brothers also drove for Parry's

This Volvo 6wl stock lorry H385MTX is to be seen serving local markets on a regular basis.

This 'E' Series ERF 6-wheeler F749AUH with curtainsider body delivers animal feedstuffs to the farming community on behalf of BOCM Pauls.

Michael Parry washing out his ERF 6-wheeler on the Lorry Wash at Abergavenny Market.

B.W. REES & SON, CARDIFF

Benjamin Walter Rees first started collecting milk in 1929 using a car and trailer twice daily to collect churns from a single producer and deliver it to a small private dairy at Rumney, Cardiff. Thereafter he was to collect churns from the railway station, which had been transported by rail from Somerset, and haul it to Gaze, Broadway, Cardiff and Cardiff Wholesale Dairies. His first proper churn round was to come in the early 1940s using a Bedford lorry CKG316 and making collections in the Usk area. However whilst milk transport was to become the main activity in the early days he was involved in a wide range of other business, including the transport of livestock.

After the war he was to become transport manager for the Seed Merchants Noah Rees & Griffin Ltd of Working Street, Cardiff, who operated a fleet of five motor lorries carrying out deliveries of hay, straw, fertilizer and cattle feed to the farming community. Whilst his own lorries were employed on milk transport in the mornings, additional revenue was earned hauling for Noah Rees & Griffin in the afternoon.

He established himself at 'Glenside', Old Hill, St. Mellons, Monmouthshire, which was situated within easy reach of Cardiff. Expansion was rapid and collections were carried out over a wide area of South East Wales, and eventually even further afield. With the growth of the business the milk transport was thereafter based at 385B, Newport Road, Cardiff – the old Taff Vale Railway yard.

Carrying out repairs inhouse, and offering engineering services, and soon becoming involved in tractor sales and servicing, he opened a Welding and Heavy Engineering workshop at 308, Newport Road, Cardiff, and this was to be an important part of the business.

His son Graham served his time in engineering with Perkins Engines at Peterborough, and on completion of his apprenticeship joined his father in the firm in 1958.

On December 1, 1969 they commenced bulk collections of milk from selected farms, initially with a tanker hired from the Milk Marketing Board. The transition from churn to bulk collection was a gradual process only achieved when all farms were fitted with the necessary equipment. However, this was eventually carried out, and they collected their last churns on January 31, 1979. By this time they were operating a modern purpose built fleet of tankers.

Sadly in April 1977 Benjamin Rees passed away, but Graham was to be assisted by his son Howard and daughter Helen.

At this time they were also using articulated bulk tankers for deliveries from dairy to manufacturing outlets, and the general haulage business was expanded. It was not unusual to see Rees vehicles involved in steel transport from British Steel at Llanwern and on container traffic throughout the country.

In 1991 Graham decided to retire, and in consequence sold the business to Express Dairies. His son is involved in landscaping, and established Duck Automotive Ltd at Portskewitt, initially operating an ERF 6wl lorry transporting wooden sectional buildings. Problems with access on this work dictated the need for smaller 4wl flatbeds, and currently two Leylands are being used.

Thus, whilst the familiar green and yellow vehicles of the B.W. Rees & son fleet have disappeared, the family still keep an interest in transport.

Fleet List

Index No.	Fleet No.	Vehicle	Notes
–	11	Fiat	No details
–	12	Reo dropside/flat	New
BLT---	13	Bedford dropside/flat	–
–	14	Ford flat	–
CKG316	15	Bedford OWLD dropside/flat	New under MOT license on 14.1.1942
CKG635	16	Bedford OWLD dropside/flat	New under MOT license on 23.5.1945
CKG269	17	Bedford OWLD dropside/flat	From British Road Services
CKG233	18	Bedford OWLD dropside/flat	From British Road Services

Index No.	Fleet No.	Vehicle	Notes
AUD835	19	Bedford OWLD dropside/flat	From BRS Parcels
FTX865	20	Bedford 'O' type flat	–
EBO994	21	Bedford dropside/flat	From Joe Sheppard
HTG983	22	Bedford OWLD flat	From Boltons, Merthyr
BUH313	23	Albion KL127 flat	From British Road Services
JWO781	24	Albion Chieften flat	New from Watts, Lydney
NPJ416	25	Commer Superpoise flat	From N.J. Counsell
RPB485	26	Commer Superpoise flat	From N.J. Counsell
GDW18?	27	Austin Loadstar flat	From N.J. Counsell
MWO736	28	Bedford A5 flat	From N.J. Counsell
MKG338	29	Ford 4D dropside flat	–
HAX814	30	Morris Commercial flat	New from City Motors, Cardiff
LKG32	31	Morris Commercial flat	New from City Motors, Cardiff
SAX754	32	Morris Commercial flat	New from City Motors, Cardiff
RWO285	33	Austin flat	New from Howells, Cardiff
UAX367	34	Morris BMC 7 ton flat	New from City Motors, Cardiff
DUH483	35	Morris canvas/dropside	From Moreland
HUH366	36	Ford Cost Cutter canvas/dropside	From Moreland
OAX740	37	BMC 7 ton flat	From City Motors, Cardiff
XWO985	38	Bedford 'S' type 7 ton flat	New from Arlington Motors, Cardiff
XWO986	39	Bedford 'J' type 7 ton flat	New from Arlington Motors, Cardiff
WBO864	40	Bedford TK flat	New from Arlington Motors, Cardiff
WTG546	41	Bedford C6 flat	–
MBO241	42	Bedford 'S' type flat	–
216CWO	43	Bedford TK flat	New from Arlington Motors, Cardiff
JUH775	44	Morris canvas/dropside	–
WTX422	45	Bedford C6 flat	–
6403DD	46	Albion Reiver 6wl flat	From Martin Raven
LUH457	47	Bedford D5 canvas/dropside	–
CBO761B	48	Bedford TK flat	New from Arlington Motors, Cardiff
KKG374	49	Bedford A5 flat	From Robinson David, Cardiff
GAX670C	50	Ford D750 flat	New from A.E. Harris
308RNY	51	Bedford TK flat	From Terry Smith
HAX541D	52	Ford D600 flat	New from A.E. Harris
JWO213D	53	Ford D600 flat	New from A.E. Harris
UBC459	54	Ford Trader 6D flat	–
LWO281E	55	Ford D600 flat	New from R.J. Bown

Index No.	Fleet No.	Vehicle	Notes
MAX193E	56	Ford D750 flat	New from R.J. Bown
AKG27B	57	Ford 'K' type 4D flat	–
MAX777E	58	Ford D700 flat	New from R.J. Bown
1271N	59	Bedford J5 flat	From Massey Ferguson
NWO666F	60	Ford D750 flat	New from R.J. Bown
OAX800F	61	Ford D750 flat	New from R.J. Bown
PAX888F	62	Ford D750 flat	New from R.J. Bown
154GXK	63	Bedford TK box van	–
RWO456G	64	Ford D750 flat	New from R.J. Bown
TAX461G	65	Bedford TK flat	New from Arlington Motors, Cardiff
UAX11H	66	Bedford TK flat	New from Atlas Garages, Newport
VAX880H	67	Albion CD56 tanker	New from C.V. Sales, Cardiff
WAX700J	68	Albion CD56 tanker	New from Arlington Motors, Cardiff
YAX400J	69	Albion CD56 tanker	New from Arlington Motors, Cardiff
BWO333K	70	Albion CD56 tanker	New from Arlington Motors, Cardiff
CWO888K	71	ERF 54G tanker	New from South Wales Commercials, Newport
EAX333K	72	ERF 54G tanker	New from South Wales Commercials, Newport
EWO88K	73	Ford D750 flat	New from R.J. Bown
NWO4M	74	Leyland tanker	New from Arlington Motors, Cardiff
RAX412M	75	ERF 54G tanker	New from South Wales Commercials, Newport
GHB226N	76	ERF 64G tanker	New from South Wales Commercials, Newport
WUD691H	77	Albion CD21 tanker	From Bury's Oxford
PTG636R	78	ERF 54G tanker	ERF rebuild
RDW891R	79	ERF 54G tanker	ERF rebuild
SNY260S	80	Seddon Atkinson tanker	New from Telford Motors, Cardiff
FNY391K	81	ERF 64P flat	–
HHA177D	82	ERF 64G tanker	–
XHB7T	83	ERF 64G tanker	ERF rebuild from 24 ton artic.
AAX452T	84	ERF 64G tanker	ERF rebuild from 24 ton artic.
AHB18T	85	ERF 64G tanker	ERF rebuild from 24 ton artic.
NTU594H	86	ERF 54G tanker	–
EUD911K	87	Albion CD21 tanker	From Bury's, Oxford
NHR541M	88	Leyland tanker	–
EKG832V	89	ERF 64G tanker	ERF rebuild from 24 ton artic.

Index No.	Fleet No.	Vehicle	Notes
TDW598J	90	ERF 6LXB articulated tractor unit	From D. Gillard, Cwmbran
FW112K	91	Albion tanker	From Bury's Oxford
AYB298H	92	Atkinson articulated tractor unit	–
MAX778X	93	ERF 64G tanker	ERF rebuild from 24 ton artic.
RHO791P	94	Scammell Crusader articulated tractor unit	–
TBO590S	95	Ford D1000 articulated tractor unit	Left Hand drive
XFR394R	96	ERF articulated tractor unit	–
ROA431M	97	Seddon tanker	–
MCB321R	98	ERF 64G flat	–
OWO384Y	99	Mercedes tanker	New from Euro Commercials, Cardiff
NWO628X	100	Dennis tanker	New from Dennis
SAX654Y	101	Mercedes tanker	New from Euro Commercials, Cardiff
KFS711T	102	ERF articulated tractor unit	–
A734WBO	103	ERF 'M' series tanker	New from South Wales Commercials, Newport
CAC603T	104	Bedford TM flat	–
TKG745S	105	Volvo F86 articulated tractor unit	–
B825BNY	106	Volvo F16 tanker	New from Griffin Mill
C670FHB	107	Daf drawbar tanker	New from Cardiff Daf
VAO135S	108	ERF articulated tractor unit	–
VAO136S	109	ERF articulated tractor unit	–
PFU443S	110	Leyland Marathon articulated tractor unit	–
BAL241T	111	Leyland Marathon articulated tractor unit	–
GYM164N	112	Ford canvas/dropside	–
GUJ698V	113	Leyland Roadtrain articulated tractor unit	–
NHU874Y	114	Mercedes articulated tractor unit	–
WVG499X	115	Volvo drawbar tanker	Converted from tractor unit
OFB839Y	116	Mercedes articulated tractor unit	–
A409VBO	117	Mercedes 6wl tanker	From Euro Commercials, Cardiff
GBO630W	118	Ford D series box van	–
D752KWO	119	Mercedes 1628 articulated tractor unit	New from Euro Commercials, Cardiff
B915ATG	120	Mercedes 2028 articulated tractor unit	From Euro Commercials, Cardiff

Index No.	Fleet No.	Vehicle	Notes
C391HUH	121	Mercedes 1628 articulated tractor unit	From Euro Commercials, Cardiff
B916ATG	122	Mercedes articulated tractor unit	From Euro Commercials, Cardiff
LTX267X	123	Volvo F10 articulated tractor unit	–
PGS984W	124	Foden articulated tractor unit	–
PGS989W	125	Foden articulated tractor unit	–
JWS607X	126	ERF articulated tractor unit	–
D635GHU	127	ERF articulated tractor unit	–
AKH270X	128	Daf articulated tractor unit	–
MHA157V	129	Foden articulated tractor unit	–
GSA275V	130	Leyland Flat/Hiab 6x4	–
MOF91X	131	Daf 6wl flat	–
B874XOU	132	Mercedes fridge box	–
D358---	133	Mercedes fridge box	–

This Reo 4wl dropside lorry was supplied new to B.W. Rees immediately before the Second World War by Richards Bros., Mountjoy Street, Newport, where it is photographed. It was soon requisitioned by the Government and had to be delivered at Hereford. The Reo was a popular vehicle being imported from the United States. The Reo company's name was taken from its founder Mr. R. E. Olds initials. An earlier venture being named Oldsmobile.

A young Graham Rees is seen with the Bedford OWLD – CKG635. This vehicle was bought new in May, 1945, under a Ministry License. His Welsh Cob can be seen in the background.

This Bedford OWLD, AUD835 was bought at auction from BRS Parcels where it had seen service in Oxford.

Opposite top left: This Bedford OWLD, CKG233 was bought off British Road Services.

Opposite top right: Now part of the Rees churn collection fleet, this Bedford 'O' type, EB0994 was bought from Joe Shepherd, Fruit Merchants of Custom House Street, Cardiff.

Opposite bottom: This Albion KL127, BUH313 (Fleet No: 23) was fitted with a Gardner 4LK engine and returned the amazing fuel consumption figures of over 20 mpg. It was new to Lansdown Motors of Cardiff, but B.W. Rees bought it from BRS.

Top: A Bedford 'O' type, FTX865 loaded with milk churns.

Above: Bedford 'O' type, EB0994 with two Bedford OWLD's HTG983 and AUD835. All being employed on milk churns collection.

Opposite: Three of four vehicles bought from N. J. Counsell, of Newport, which had previously been used on milk churn collection. Commer Superpoise flats NPJ416 and RPB485, and a Bedford A5, MW0736.

Above left: This Bedford OWLD (22) HTG983 was bought from Boltons of Merthyr Tydfil.

Above right: This Albion Chieftain, JW0781 (Fleet No: 24) was bought new in 1951 from Watts of Lydney.

This Morris BMC flat, UAX367 was bought new from City Motors, Cardiff.

Bought new in 1957, this Austin 4-wheeler RW0285 came from Howells, Cardiff. (Also pictured below).

Austin flat, LKG32 (31) came new from City Motors, Cardiff.

HAX814 a Morris Commercial was supplied by City Motors, Cardiff.

Driver Brian Pretty is seen loading milk churns onto the Morris 4-wheeler, UAX367 (34) at The Home Farm, Tredegar House, Newport.

A small part of the B. W. Rees & Son fleet employed on churn collection shown at their St. Mellons premises – Morris LKG32 (31), Bedford 'S' type XW0985 (38), Bedford TK WB0864 (40) and Austin RW0285 (33) with Ford 4D MKG338 (29) in the background to the right.

Bedford 'J' type XW0986 (39) shown at Newport Road, Cardiff.

This Bedford TK – WB0864 (40) was fitted with small wheels and tyres.

This 1961 Bedford TK – 216CWO (43) was supplied new by Arlington Motors, Cardiff.

This Albion Reiver 6wl flat 6403DD was employed on general haulage.

Morris canvas/dropside, JUH775 was employed on the engineering/welding side of the business. Vehicles so employed were finished in a maroon livery, whilst haulage vehicles were green with the later edition of yellow cab trim for higher conspicuity.

Ford D750, GAX670C (50) employed on churn collection.

On December 1, 1969 B.W. Rees & Son commenced bulk collections of milk from selected farms, initially with a tanker hired from the Milk Marketing Board. In 1970/71 they bought their first tankers, four Albion CD56s. YAX400J is shown at their Cardiff depot.

This pair of ERF 54G ('A' Series) milk tankers CW0888K and EAX333K entered service in 1972. ERF was to be a much favoured vehicle in the Rees fleet for this work.

Overleaf: The Gardner-engined (5LW-100) ERF, CWO888K is shown negotiating narrow lanes in Monmouthshire.

Page 79: Bulk Milk tanker CW0888K is making an on-farm collection.

B.W. Rees & Son Ltd. bought four of these ERF tankers new before the manufacturer discontinued the chassis in favour of a heavier model unsuitable for their work. They managed to purchase two modern vehicles in tanker form from other owners. Wanting more of this specification they bought two 5LW rigids and five 6LW 24 ton articulated tractor units which they had rebuilt by ERF into the original specification, and entered service re-registered.

Above: Three generations – Benjamin Walter Rees, son Graham and grandson Howard with the first ERF.

Opposite bottom: This pair of Albion CD21 tankers EUD911K and WUD691H were bought from Bury's Transport of Whitney, Oxfordshire. They were used to transport liquid egg from Cardiff locally and to Rogerstone and Leeds for the baking industry.

Opposite top: Supplied new by South Wales Commercials, Newport, the fourth ERF was the first with the Gardner 6LW (120) engine. The vehicle had been allocated the index number SAX698N prior to entering service, and changes in the registrations system prior to licensing meant that it actually entered service as GHB226N.

SEDDON
ATKINSON
200
TRUCK
OF THE YEAR

(80)

B.W. REES & SON

Transport
Contractors

CARDIFF

Phones —
32152/3
77141

This Seddon Atkinson 4wl milk tanker SNY260S (Fleet No:80) was supplied new by Telford Motors, Cardiff, in 1977. It was not a success in service and no others of its type were acquired.

B. W. Rees & Son Ltd. were engineers in their own right and whilst they often bought new vehicles, they were not afraid to buy secondhand. They sometimes bought vehicles which bordered on scrap, and having the capability rebuilt them from bottom up. Part of their business was involved with supplying agricultural tractors and this often meant taking-in part exchange vehicles which would be rebuilt and refurbished before resale. Engineers they were, but they were specialist welders – no job being too big or difficult.

Opposite top left: This Leyland 4wl tanker NHR541M was bought secondhand and was in such good condition that it was left in its blue livery.

Opposite top right: This ERF with Gardner 6LW engine started life as a 24 ton articulated tractor unit. It was bought by B. W. Rees & Son, and sent back to the ERF factory where it was completely rebuilt as a 4 wheel rigid mounted with a tank and re-registered as EKG832V.

Left: Graham Rees with daughter Helen and son Howard. The vehicle was MAX778X (93), the last of the seven vehicles rebuilt by ERF for Rees.

Above: This ERF with Gardner 6LXB (180) engine TDW598J was their first articulated tractor unit. It was bought knowingly with a seized drive axle, and rebuilt in-house. It was used to transport milk and cream from dairy to manufacturing outlets.

Whilst B. W. Rees & Son Ltd. maintained their on-farm collection of milk in bulk, there was a demand for maximum capacity tankers to transport milk, cream and other food products. At the same time the opportunity was taken, as they became involved with articulated vehicles, to expand into other work. They had always carried out some general haulage work but from 1980 were hauling steel, containers with lowloader and other work. This Scammell Crusader RH0791P (above) was acquired. The vehicle is shown in the lower picture carrying a vessel on a step-frame semi-trailer.

This ERF 'B' Series tractor unit KFS711T was used on Freightliner work.

This Mercedes tanker OWO384Y was delivered new in 1981 by Euro Commercials, Cardiff.

This Ford D1000 tractor unit TB0590S (95) was fitted with left hand drive steering.

ERF 'B' Series tractor unit VR0136S coupled to a triaxle tanker trailer.

This ERF 4wl bulk milk tanker A734WBO fitted with a Perkins T6354.4 engine. It was delivered new by South Wales Commercials, Newport. It was one of three identical vehicles, the other two going to Wincanton Transport and the Milk Marketing Board.

A Volvo 4wl tanker B825BNY came new from Griffin Mill Garage.

Bought new from Euro Commercials, Cardiff, in 1986 their Mercedes 1968 articulated tractor unit D752KWO is shown (Above) operating as a low-loader, and (below) with a tank trailer.

Mercedes tractor unit NHU874Y (114)

Daf 2800 articulated tractor unit AKH250X (128)

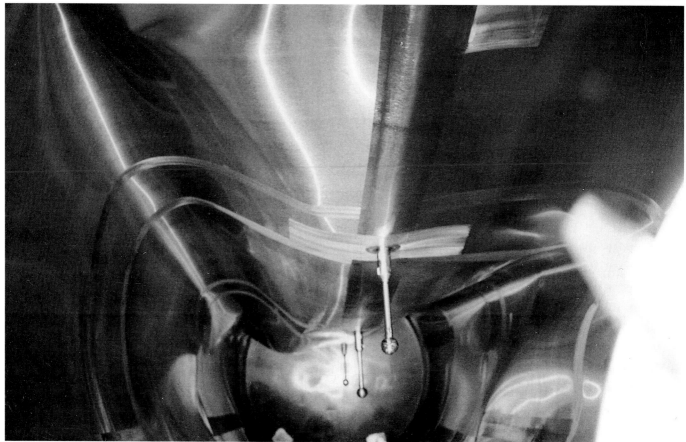

Opposite top: External view of tank trailer which has imploded.

Opposite bottom: Internal view of same trailer showing extent of damage.

When the stainless steel tanks are cleaned following discharge of cargo they are cleaned under considerable heat with fluid – detergent and water, if the tank is not ventilated sufficiently to take account of this extreme heat the tank will implode as in the photographs, causing considerable damage.

Above: Mercedes 1720 tractor unit F555YWO on demonstration to B. W. Rees & Son Ltd. from Euro Commercials, Cardiff.

Volvo drawbar tanker, WVG499X. Originally an articulated tractor unit, it has been stretched to convert it for drawbar operation. One of the first drawbar milk tanker outfits in the country.

Mercedes 6wl tanker C532JBO. The tank has been converted from that originally operated as a four wheeler.

ERF 'C' Series tractor unit JWS607X (126).

Graham Rees with his son and daughter with the Scammell Highwayman recovery vehicle.

Two views of Mercedes 1628 tractor unit C391HUH (121). In the lower photograph it is seen at Llanwern Steelworks.

ERF 'E' Series D635GHU (127) loading steel coils at the British Steel Corporation Llanwern Steelworks. Graham Rees is seen in the upper view.

ROBERTS TRANSPORT (ROSS ROADWAYS), WHITCHURCH, ROSS-ON-WYE

The family owned business of Roberts Transport, also known as Ross Roadways, was established on February 1, 1968, when brothers Anthony and Graham Roberts entered into partnership and acquired an eight year old Foden 8 wheel bulk tipper. Anthony was a plant operator and initially kept his job, whilst Graham who had driven for Richard Read of Longhope in the Forest of Dean was to drive the newly purchased vehicle.

The Foden was normally employed hauling foundry coke from South Wales to the Midlands areas and reloading gypsum or coal back into South Wales. When not on the road the vehicle was parked at Glyn Morris Transport's Kilcot Garage at Gorsley, but eventually they were to find suitable space to park it near the family home at Llandinabo near Wormelow.

After a year they replaced the Foden with a more modern Atkinson 8 wheel tipper which had been new to Hansons of Wakefield, and being painted green and red, they adopted these colours as the Roberts livery. At this time Anthony gave up his job, and the two brothers operated the vehicle by day and night.

In 1972 they moved their operating base to premises at Millpond Lane, Ross-on-Wye, and the following year, now owning three vehicles, were joined in the partnership by brothers Haydn, who looked after the maintenance and Terry who organised the loads and did the paperwork.

During 1973 they purchased their first new vehicle, an Atkinson tractor unit at a cost of £6,000 plus VAT from Praills of Hereford, and whilst maintaining their bulk tipper work, expanded into steel haulage from British Steel at Llanwern and Orb Electrical Steels at Newport.

Further growth in the business came in 1982 when they took over H.S. Williams Haulage of Ross-on-Wye and its fleet of four articulated outfits, and expanded into the haulage of timber from the Forest of Dean and raised access flooring tiles from Hereford.

They quickly outgrew their Ross-on-Wye premises and as a result in 1987 moved to purpose built premises at Whitchurch, not far distant from Ross-on-Wye, and adjacent to the A40 dual carriageway with its excellent links to the motorway network.

The four brothers currently operate a modern maximum GVW fleet of articulated tractor units and semi-trailers, with their main activities continuing to be steel and bulk tipper haulage.

Fleet List

Index No.	Vehicle	Notes
1271RF	1960 Foden 8wl tipper	Gardner 150, 12 speed gearbox, payload 14 tons. Purchased from Thornbury, Nr. Bristol.
HWX387C	1965 Atkinson 8wl tipper	Gardner 150, David Brown 6 speed gearbox, Kirkstall double drive, payload 14 tons. Purchased from Stanley Hughes Commercials at Cleckheaton, ex-Hansons of Wakefield; the vehicles was green and red, and this was adopted as the Roberts livery.
OVJ888G	1969 ERF tractor unit	Gardner 180, David Brown 6 speed gearbox, Eaton 2 speed axle, payload 21.5 tons. Purchased from Trevor Oakley, Hereford; 1976 written off at Monmouth.
AWU122G	1969 Atkinson Mk 2 8wl tipper	Gardner 180, David Brown 6 speed gearbox, Kirkstall double drive, payload 16 tons. Purchased from Comberhill Garages, Wakefield, ex-Hansons of Wakefield.
CVJ508L	1973 Atkinson Mk 2 tractor unit	Roberts first new vehicle, costing £6,000 plus VAT; Cummins 220, 10 speed Fuller gearbox, Kirkstall rear axle, payload 21 tons. Purchased from Praills of Hereford.

Index No.	Vehicle	Notes
JAX968L	1973 Volvo F88 tractor unit	Payload 20 tons. Purchased from Griffin Garages.
GCJ642N	1974 Volvo F88 tractor unit	Payload 20 tons. Purchased from Gammonds Transport, Hereford.
TTD174L	1972 Seddon tractor unit	Payload 21 tonnes. Purchased from Robert Wynn & Sons Ltd., Newport; new to John Ancliffe, Manchester.
BMX140H	1970 Atkinson Mk 2 tractor unit	Payload 21 tonnes. Purchased from Renwicks, Lydbrook, Glos.
NEP744R	1976 Seddon Atkinson 8wl tipper	Gardner 180, David Brown 6 speed gearbox, Eaton double drive, payload 19 tonnes. Purchased from B.A. Rogers, Skewen.
UCJ965S	1978 Seddon Atkinson tractor unit	Gardner 180, David Brown 6 speed gearbox, Eaton 2 speed axle, payload 20 tonnes. Purchased new from Praills of Hereford.
HDG286V	1980 ERF B Series tractor unit	Cummins E290, Fuller 9 speed gearbox, Kirkstall rear axle, payload 20 tonnes. Purchased new from Richard Read (Commercials) Ltd., Longhope, Glos. Later converted to a 6wl unit for operation at 38 tonnes gross. Vehicle privately preserved.
PHB247R	1977 Seddon Atkinson tractor unit	Gardner 240, Fuller 9 speed gearbox, Eaton rear axle, payload 20 tonnes. Purchased from Brian Chilton, South Wales.
WAD12X	1982 Seddon Atkinson tractor unit	Gardner 240, Fuller 9 speed gearbox, Eaton rear axle, payload 20 tonnes. Purchased new from Ryland Trucks, Dudley.
XFH34S	1978 ERF B Series tractor unit	Cummins 250, Fuller 9 speed gearbox, Kirkstall rear axle, payload 20 tonnes. Purchased in 1982 with the takeover of H.S. Williams Haulage Ltd., Ross-on-Wye.
OFH213R	1976 Ford Transcontinental tractor unit	Cummins 335, Fuller gearbox, payload 20 tonnes. Purchased in 1982 with the takeover of H.S. Williams Haulage Ltd., Ross-on-Wye.
HDG279V	1979 ERF B Series tractor unit	Rolls Royce 265, Fuller 9 speed gearbox, Kirkstall rear axle, payload 20 tonnes. Purchased in 1982 with the takeover of H.S. Williams Haulage Ltd., Ross-on-Wye.
KCJ820P	1975 ERF A Series tractor unit	Rolls Royce 280, Fuller gearbox. Purchased in 1982 with the takeover of H.S. Williams Haulage Ltd., Ross-on-Wye; not used – sold.
MUX639P	1976 ERF B Series tractor unit	Gardner 240, Fuller 9 speed gearbox, Eaton rear axle, payload 20 tonnes. Purchased from Potters of Welshpool.
MUE74P	1976 Seddon Atkinson tractor unit	Cummins 250, Fuller 9 speed gearbox, Group axle, payload 21 tonnes. Purchased at auction, ex-British Gas.
NPG287P	1976 Atkinson Mk 2 tractor unit	Cummins 250, Fuller 9 speed gearbox, Group axle, payload 21 tonnes. Purchased from Wye Commercials, Ross-on-Wye.

Index No.	Vehicle	Notes
A512GAD	1983 ERF C Series 6wl tractor unit	Cummins E290, Fuller 9 speed gearbox, Kirkstall rear axle, payload 24 tonnes. Purchased new from Richard Read (Commercials) Ltd., Longhope, Glos. – the first 38 tonner sold by them.
B904GAO	1984 ERF C Series 6wl tractor unit	Cummins E320, Fuller gearbox, 40 tonnes GVW. Purchased from Scunthorpe.
B262TVJ	1985 Seddon Atkinson 401 6wl tractor unit	Cummins E320, Fuller 13 speed gearbox, 40 tonnes GVW. Purchased new from Praills of Hereford.
A739OFO	1983 Foden 6wl tractor unit	Cummins E290, Fuller 9 speed gearbox, 38 tonnes GVW. Purchased from C.G. Griffiths, Kington.
C598SVT	1985 ERF C Series 4wl tractor unit	Cummins E320, Fuller 9 speed gearbox, 40 tonnes. From Foulkes, Appleby Magna.
E426EFO	1987 Foden 6wl tractor unit	Cummins E320, Fuller 13 speed gearbox, Eaton double drive, 40 tonnes GVW. Purchased new from Fairwood Trucks, Swansea.
D779EDD	1986 ERF E Series 6wl tractor unit	Cummins E320, Eaton twin splitter gearbox, 40 tonnes GVW. Purchased from M.C. Wilson, Hereford.
G344RCJ	1989 ERF E Series 6wl tractor unit	Cummins E320, Eaton twin splitter gearbox, 40 tonnes GVW. Purchased new from Richard Read (Commercials) Ltd., Longhope, Glos.
H499XCJ	1990 Seddon Atkinson Strato 6wl tractor unit	Cummins 365, Eaton twin splitter gearbox, 40 tonnes GVW. Purchased new from Hernward Commercials, Newport.
F87CEP	1989 ERF E Series 6wl tractor unit	Cummins E320, Eaton twin splitter gearbox, 40 tonnes GVW. Purchased from Potters of Welshpool.
F111EEP	1988 ERF E Series 6wl tractor unit	Cummins 400, Fuller 9 speed gearbox, 40 tonnes GVW. Purchased from Potters of Welshpool.
N328WVJ	1995 Foden 6wl tractor unit	Perkins 375, Fuller 13 speed gearbox, Eaton double drive, 40 tonnes GVW. Purchased new from Fairwood Trucks, Swansea.
M656MVP	1995 ERF EC 6wl tractor unit	Cummins 340, Eaton twin splitter gearbox, 41 tonnes GVW. Purchased from Richardsons of Rugeley.
M448VER	1994 ERF EC 6wl tractor unit	Cummins 340, Eaton twin splitter gearbox, 41 tonnes GVW. Purchased from Brian Harris Transport, Devon.
R646FEU	1997 Foden 6wl tractor unit	Perkins 380, double drive, 44 tonnes GVW. Purchased from Dunkerley Transport.
W159UCJ	2000 Foden 6wl tractor unit	Cummins 405, 16 speed gearbox, 44 tonnes GVW. Purchased new from Fairwood Commercials, Swansea.
W361XTH	2000 Foden 6wl tractor unit	Cummins 440, 16 speed gearbox, 44 tonnes GVW. Purchased from Fairwood Commercials, Swansea.

Index No.	Vehicle	Notes
Y83KJA	2001 ERF EX 6wl tractor unit	Cummins 410, 16 speed gearbox, 44 tonnes GVW. Purchased from Wye Commercials, Ross-on-Wye.
T345LKK	1999 ERF EC 6wl tractor unit	Cummins 420, 16 speed gearbox, 44 tonnes GVW. Purchased from Wye Commercials, Ross-on-Wye.
S285NTP	1998 ERF EC 6wl tractor unit	Cummins 420, 16 speed gearbox, 44 tonnes GVW. Purchased from Wye Commercials, Ross-on-Wye.
VX04CDU	2004 ERF ECT 6wl tractor unit	Cummins 420, 16 speed gearbox, 44 tonnes GVW. Purchased new from ERF.

Roberts Transport's first vehicle in 1968 was this eight year old Foden bulk tipper 1271RF which Graham Roberts drove. It was normally used hauling foundry coke out of South Wales to the Midlands.

In 1969 Graham and Anthony Roberts replaced the earlier vehicle with this 1965 Gardner-engined Atkinson bulk tipper HWX387C.

The Atkinson tipper HWX387C which had been new to R. Hanson & Son Ltd., Wakefield, was operated by night and day by brothers Graham and Anthony.

The arrival of this ERF LV articulated outfit OVJ888G marked the brothers entry into steel transport.

Roberts Transport (Ross Roadways) first new vehicle was this Atkinson Mk.2 tractor unit CVJ508L from Praills of Hereford. Its arrival in 1973 coincided with Haydn and Terry joining their brothers in the partnership.

When bought new in 1980 from Richard Read (Commercial) Ltd., this ERF 'B ' Series tractor unit HDG286V was a 4x2, but it was subsequently converted to a 6x2 vehicle for operation at 38 tonnes GVW. The vehicle is now privately preserved.

Seen on the M6 Motorway at Preston in October, 1976 was this modern Volvo F88 GCJ642N with tandem-axled bulk tipper trailer.

108

Roberts Transport (Ross Roadways) had been in existence for 14 years when in 1982 they took over the old established business of H. S. Williams Haulage of Ross-on-Wye and its fleet of four tractor units and trailers. Thereafter they expanded into the haulage of timber from the Forest of Dean and raised access flooring tiles from Hereford. Half their fleet was operated in the blue and red colours of H. S. Williams, a policy which was to continue for a further fifteen years. H. S. Williams Haulage is a wholly-owned subsidiary of the Roberts business and whilst today no vehicles carry its colours, it still exists.

Opposite top: This ERF 'C' Series tractor unit A512GAD fitted with a Cummins E290 engine was bought new in 1983 from Richard Read (Commercials) Ltd., Longhope – the first 38 tonner sold by them. It carries the colours of H. S. Williams. Seddon Atkinson WAD12X in the Roberts colours, acquired new in 1982 from Ryland Trucks of Dudley.

Opposite centre: Yard scene showing ERF, Foden and Seddon Atkinson units in the colours of both Roberts and Williams.

Opposite bottom and above left: This 1985 Seddon Atkinson 401 6x2 tractor unit B262TVJ was bought new from Praills of Hereford.

Above right: This 1976 Atkinson Mk2 tractor unit NPG287P with Cummins 250 engine was bought from Wye Commercials, Ross-on-Wye.

Opposite and above: In 1987 the firm moved to purpose built premises at Whitchurch, near Ross-on-Wye.

Above: Three units of the fleet at the Whitchurch premises. An ERF 'C' Series B904GAO of 1984 is seen with a 1990 Seddon Atkinson Strato H499XCJ and Foden E426EFO of 1987.

This Foden 6x4 tractor unit E426EFO with Cummins E320 engine operated at 40 tonnes GVW. It was supplied new in 1987 by Fairwood Trucks, Swansea.

Foden E426EFO is shown at Avonmouth Docks.

This Foden 6wl tractor unit N328WVJ was supplied new by Fairwood Trucks, Swansea.

Above: ERF 'C' Series tractor unit C598SVT had a Cummins E320 engine.
Below: ERF 'E' Series 6x2 tractor unit D779EDD operated at 40 tonners GVW.

Foden's N328WVJ and E426EFO outside a pair of ERFs F111EEP and D779EDD at Royal Portbury Dock waiting to load soya.

ERF 'E' Series D770EDD and ERF 'C' Series C598SVT unloading soya at the Sun Valley Feed Mill at Allensmore, Herefordshire.

ERF 'E' Series G344RCJ with curtainsider trailer.

Foden tractor unit W159UCJ was bought new in 2000 from Fairwood Commercials, Swansea. The vehicle is being loaded with sugar beet.

P.M. HEATON PUBLISHING

Paul Heaton was born at New Inn, Pontypool, in 1944 and was educated at Greenlawn Junior School in New Inn and the Wern Secondary School at Sebastopol. At fifteen he commenced employment, at first in a local store and then with a builder's merchant. A year later he was appointed as a Deck Cadet in the Merchant Navy, with the Lamport & Holt Line of Liverpool, and served in their vessels *Chatham, Constable* and *Romney* usually in the Brazil and River Plate trades. He joined the Monmouthshire Constabulary (now Gwent) in 1963, and served at Abergavenny, Cwmbran, Newport, the Traffic Department, the Motor Cycle Section, as the Press Liaison Officer, and for five years represented Inspectors for the whole of Wales nationally on the Joint Central Committee of the Police Federation. He was promoted to sergeant in 1974 and Inspector in 1982. On his retirement he served as Market Inspector with the RSPCA for eight years and at the same time was Landlord of a Public House for three years. He has always maintained an interest in maritime history and in transport generally, and has had the following books published:

Reardon Smith 1905-1980 (1980)
The Baron Glanely of St. Fagans and W.J. Tatem Ltd., with H.S. Appleyard (1980)
The 'Redbrook', A Deep-Sea Tramp (1981) four editions
The 'Usk' Ships (1982) two editions
The Abbey Line (1983)
Kaye, Son & Co. Ltd., with K. O'Donoghue (1983)
Reardon Smith Line 1984) two editions
The South American Saint Line (1985)
Welsh Blockade Runners in the Spanish Civil War (1985)
Lamport & Holt (1986) two editions
Tatems of Cardiff (1987)
Booth Line (1987)
Jack Billmeir, Merchant Shipowner (1989)
Welsh Shipping, Forgotten Fleets (1989)
The Gallant Ship 'Stephen Hopkins' with R.J. Witt (1990)
Palm Line, with Laurence Dunn (1994)
Not All Coppers Are...! (1994)
Wynns – The First 100 Years for John Wynn (1995) three editions
Wynns – The Last 20 Years for John Wynn (1996)
L.C. Lewis, Heavy Haulage (1996)
Wynns Overseas first draft for John Wynn (1998)
The Wynns Fleet – 120 Years of Road Haulage (2003)
Lamport & Holt Line (2004)
Road Transport Gwent (2004)
Road Transport – The Read Story (2005)
Road Transport Monmouthshire (2005)
Road Transport Wales & Border (2005)